Women in Salisbury Cathedral Close

Sarum Studies 5

Jane Howells
Ruth Newman

Sarum Chronicle
recent historical research
on Salisbury & district

Portrait of Barbara Townsend painted by Alfred Weigall in the 1870s. This picture originally had a dark background but when Rex Whistler saw it in the 1930s his offer to re-paint that was accepted. Mompesson House was incomplete (there are no glazing bars) when he was killed in action in Normandy. The locket she is wearing was dark purple blue enamel with a diamond, a bridesmaid gift (courtesy of Robert Longmore, David Cousins and the National Trust).

Contents

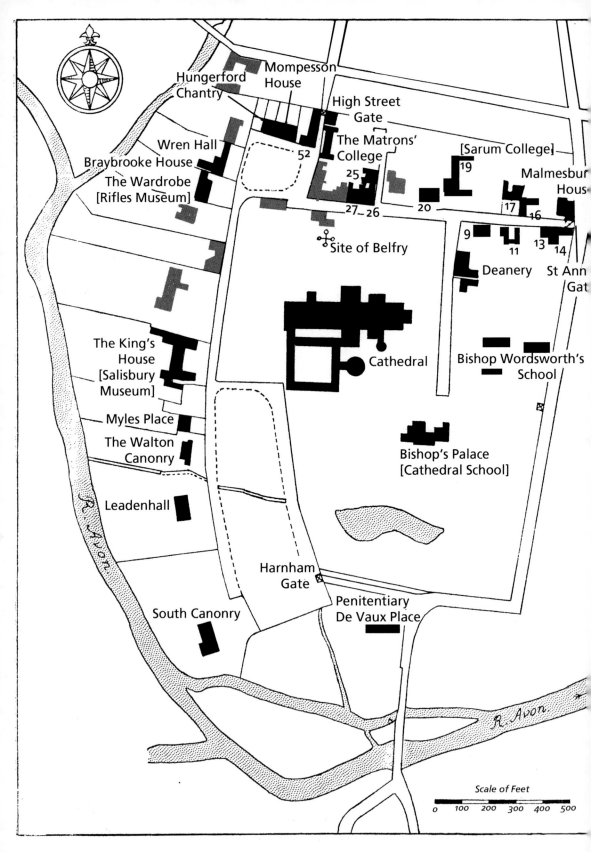

Buildings in Salisbury Cathedral Close (John Chandler)

Foreword

As a Cathedral dedicated to the Virgin Mary its very stones speak of the women who have shaped the Christian faith and the life of the Cathedral and Close. On the West Front of the Cathedral Mary the mother of Jesus stands alongside female saints such as Cecilia, Agnes and Ursula. We know that women have always been present in the Cathedral and Close but history does not always record that and so this book plays an important role in reminding us that this was and is the case.

As a female Canon of the Cathedral I am inspired by the women working here today who at times have been the only women in the role, or who at times have been the first – the stonemason, glaziers, choristers, verger, the Chapter Clerk and the Dean.

We all owe a lot to those women who have gone before us and often remained in the shadows of men.

The Revd Dame Sarah Mullally
Canon Treasurer Salisbury Cathedral

Before becoming a full-time priest, Sarah Mullally was the government's Chief Nursing Officer, the most senior nurse in England. She became a Dame Commander of the British Empire in 2005 in recognition of her contribution to nursing and midwifery. In 2012 she was appointed Canon Treasurer at Salisbury Cathedral.

ISBN 978-0-9571692-4-1 ISSN: 1475-1844

How to contact us:

To order a copy phone Ruth Newman on 01722 328922 or email ruth.
tanglewood@btinternet.com

For other titles in the *Sarum Studies* series and for back issues of *Sarum Chronicle*
please contact Jane Howells on 01722 331426 or email as below.

To submit material for consideration in future editions of *Sarum Chronicle*
email Jane Howells at jane@sarum-editorial.co.uk with the words Sarum
Chronicle in the subject line.

Editorial Team: John Chandler, John Elliott, Jane Howells, Andrew Minting, Ruth
Newman, Margaret Smith

www.sarumchronicle.wordpress.com

Designed and typeset by John Elliott
Printed by Berforts Information Press

Acknowledgements

This project began as a conference walk for the West of England & South Wales Women's History Network, and comments from participants encouraged us to develop it further into first an illustrated lecture and then the book you are reading.

Special thanks are due to John Elliott for his skilful design and typesetting which have created a volume that is so visually appealing. The collections of Salisbury & South Wiltshire Museum were the source of many significant illustrations, and the Director Adrian Green and volunteer David Chilton were most accommodating in supplying the long list of images we requested.

Robin Ravilious has generously given permission to use an informal photo of her parents on honeymoon and offered additional information on Jill Furse.

Our colleagues on the Sarum Chronicle editorial team always asked challenging questions while supporting our enterprise. John Chandler's knowledge and resources were shared with characteristic generosity.

Sarah Mullally, despite her busy role as Canon Treasurer of Salisbury Cathedral, found time to write a few thoughtful words for our foreword.

Joe Newman has provided patient help and reassurance, while Laura Shapland has been a tower of strength, both proof reading and contributing ideas and technical advice from a distance.

We would like to record our appreciation of the help given by the following:

Rosemary Allen, David Cousins, Alison Crooks of Bishop Wordsworth's School, David Dawson and Heather Ault of Wiltshire Museum Devizes, Suzanne Eward, Sarah Flanaghan and Hannah Paye of Salisbury Cathedral, Godolphin School, Jenny Head, Steve Hobbs of Wiltshire and Swindon Archives, Hilary Hugh-Jones, Sue Johnson, Peter Liversage, Robert Longmore, Ash Mills, Emily Naish librarian Salisbury Cathedral, Peter Riley curator Edwin Young Collection, David Rymill of Hampshire Record Office, Karen Rudd at Mompesson House, Salisbury City Council, Peter L Smith, Steve Stephens, Jon Stone, Tim Tatton-Brown, the late Mark Walford.

Credits for the illustrations are contained in the captions. Every effort has been made to contact copyright holders, and we apologise if any have been missed.

Opposite: View of the Cathedral, Close and Bell Tower, from a print published in 1761, Hatcher 1843

Women in the Close – introduction

When thinking of personalities in Salisbury Cathedral Close it is the men who spring to mind: Christopher Wren, James Harris, John Constable and the great bishops such as John Jewel and Seth Ward. Women, however, were important from the beginning and have played an influential role in shaping the social context of the Close ever since.

Background

As Bill Bryson has written 'Salisbury Cathedral is the single most beautiful structure in England and the close around it is the most beautiful space. Every stone, every wall, every shrub is just right.'

A momentous choice was taken when the decision was made to move from

the inconvenient and inhospitable site of Old Sarum to the valley below in the early 13th century. Bishop Herbert and his more famous brother Bishop Richard Poore were instrumental in the planning, and the latter received papal blessing in 1218 to build the new Cathedral with its spacious Close on virgin land. One of the complaints about Old Sarum was the inadequate accommodation; this was rectified by the provision of an abundant site to give 'each of the canons a proper space for the erection of a dwelling-house'. It was decreed that they should build 'fair houses of stone' and Salisbury Close does indeed contain one of the most impressive groups of buildings in the country. The vast Bishop's Palace was the first recorded structure, followed by others on generous plots especially along the western side; the Close was thus a place of affluence from the start. At 83 acres it was the largest in England, and the general layout today is the same as in the Middle Ages.

On 28 April 1220, five foundation stones for the new Cathedral were laid 'in the presence of a great multitude of common folk'. This was followed, in 1258, just 38 years later, by the consecration of the building in the presence of Henry III. The cloisters, chapter house and a free standing bell tower, (the latter demolished in 1790) were constructed in the later 13th century, and the crowning glory of the spire was added in the early 14th century. The battlemented Close Wall, with its three main gateways, was built in the years 1327-42, using stones from Old Sarum, to provide protection from increasingly demanding and confident citizens outside its precinct.

With great foresight and business acumen Bishop Richard Poore realised that establishing a city alongside his Cathedral would provide both workers and revenue. New Salisbury, contemporary with the Cathedral, was planned in a grid system known as chequers. Water courses, constructed in the 1220s and 1230s, were channelled through the streets as an integral part of the initial layout, providing both water supply and drainage. By the mid 15th century the city had developed into one of the most prosperous towns in the country based on an important woollen cloth industry.

While the relationship between the townsfolk and Cathedral hierarchy was not always amicable, they were inextricably connected. People came and went through the gates for business and pleasure, benefiting from the contrasting qualities and facilities of both.

The Medieval Close

For over three centuries the Close was an almost entirely male community. However, even in its early years there were individual women who were important to the history of Salisbury Cathedral and its Close. Lady Ela and Alice Brewer will be introduced below.

Introduction

Medieval bishops had large establishments, but the majority of their employees would have been men, with perhaps just the lowly kitchen work and laundry being done by women, probably coming from the neighbouring town. In the mid 15th century, for example, only the porter at the North Gate was officially allowed to live with his wife in the Close. At the same time there were families running a few shops in the street opposite what is now the Matrons' College, but they were short-lived.

Unsettled times in the late medieval period were reflected in the morality not just of the youthful Vicars Choral whose lifestyle was questionable, but in some instances even the canons. Mistress Alicia Hoskyns was a source of gossip, frequently seen visiting William Osgodby at Braybrooke Canonry.

A century later more women lived in the Close. To a great extent they were probably a civilising influence, but they also fought their husbands' battles. A feud came before the Dean's Court between Thomas Smythe, music teacher to the choristers, and Robert Chamberlayne, the organist. The latter's wife Agnes was a strong character, and spoke on her husband's behalf, describing a violent encounter between herself and Smythe 'she toke upp one stone and did hurle the same att the sayd Thomas Smythe'.

Houses of Canon Hume and James Lacy Esq (North Canonry and the Wardrobe), Hall 1834

Married clergy

Churchmen began to take wives in the 1530s and 40s, though not always openly, in anticipation of a change in the rules on clerical celibacy. Nicholas Shaxton, Bishop of Salisbury 1535-39, was married and had at least three children. Despite many changes in church law under Henry VIII, it was not until 1549 that the new Parliament on the accession of Edward VI passed a law permitting clergymen to marry and continue with their preaching. This was revoked under Queen Mary (1553-58), and reinstated by Elizabeth in the following reign.

The clergy here in Salisbury were not in the vanguard of those taking advantage of these developments. Bishop John Coldwell in the early 1590s had a wife. His successor Henry Cotton (1598) had 19 children, and his first wife Patience is said to be buried in the Cathedral; following him was Robert Abbott (1615) who was married three times.

A genteel place to live

Over time the arrival of wives and families in the Close changed the character of households, the servants employed, the accommodation required, and the

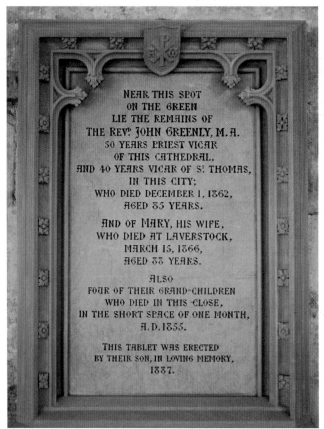

Plaque commemorating the four Greenly girls and their grandparents, North walk, Salisbury Cathedral Cloisters (photograph Peter Liversage)

atmosphere in the community. A typical image of the Close is of 18th century gentility and elegance, of quiet good taste, inhabited by a mixture of clergy families and others. Several houses were newly constructed, or largely rebuilt in the early 1700s, usually by local builders or craftsmen but influenced by the great architects, Christopher Wren and Inigo Jones.

By the mid 19th century the ratio of women to men amongst the population of the Close was 2:1. There were large households with many female servants; schools and other institutions such as the Teachers' Training College added students, staff and other employees. It was considered a safe place for spinsters and widows to live, and the Close became a socially desirable address, so lawyers and other professional men from the city moved in, with their families and servants, alongside the officers of the Cathedral.

Despite these attractions the Close was not immune from personal loss and disease. Nine residents died there in the cholera epidemic of 1849 and, in a particularly poignant tragedy, the four young granddaughters of the Rev John Greenly (Vicar of the Close and Headmaster of the Choristers' School) died of scarlet fever within the space of a month in 1855. Mary, Edith, Ellen and Rachel were all under nine years old and they appeared to be staying with their grandparents at No 18. They are commemorated in a monument in the North walk of the Cloisters with their grandparents whom they predeceased.

Girls' schools

The church has always been a provider of education, and perhaps a religious environment was considered conducive to success and security in such ventures for others. Certainly a special feature of the Close has been the number of schools located there, particularly for girls.

Small private schools can be found as early as the 17th century; for example Anne Deare, who lived in Aula le Stage from 1696–1713, is described on her Cathedral floorslab as 'the most famous mistress in the West of England for well educating and instructing young Ladys and Gentlemen'. Sarah Fielding and her sisters attended Mary Rookes's boarding school in the early 18th century. Such establishments blossomed; by the mid 18th century two girls' schools run by Mrs Ivie in the Hungerford Chantry and Mrs Smith in the King's House competed furiously for both female students and dancing masters.

Mrs Smith's 'boarding house for young ladies' in the 1760s and 1770s began an important educational link with the King's House which continued under the ambitious and energetic Mrs Voysey. In 1786 she opened a school in 'large and commodious premises' where she 'endeavours to render [young ladies] lovely to Society and pleasing to themselves'. They were to be taught 'English and French grammatically . . . and ornamental needlework at 14 guineas per annum and 1 guinea entrance'. Strict morality was adhered to, in that no books 'which are of the least dissipating tendency are admitted in the School'. Two years later Mrs Voysey was advertising, perhaps in slight desperation, in the *Salisbury Journal* that only one holiday a year should be taken and girls should stay over at Christmas, to save on the expense of travel to school and because 'the keeping of [children] at home during the recess [is] often an inconvenience'.

The Godolphin School was established in 1784 at No 25 (Elizabeth Wickens' house); its first head was Miss Gifford who had been Mrs Ivie's assistant at Hungerford Chantry. In 1837, under Miss Margaret Bazley, the school moved into the King's House. The national threat of cholera in 1848 (although it did not reach Salisbury until the following year) persuaded its owners to move from the marshy low lying area in the close to a site on Milford Hill, which it still occupies.

★★★

In 1939 G M Young wrote of 'that walled close where all the pride and piety, the peace and beauty of a vanished world seem to have made their last home under the spire of St Mary of Salisbury'. In the pages that follow women whose homes were within those walls will be introduced. Some, but not all, of their names might be familiar to readers, but the details of their lives throw light on the diverse ways they were part of the community of the Close over many centuries.

Bryson, Bill, 1996, *Notes from a Small Island*, Black Swan, 105

Cross, Claire, 2005, 'Exemplary Wives and Godly Matrons: women's contribution to the Life of York Minster between the Reformation and the Civil War', *Yorkshire Archaeological Journal*, Vol 77, 169-179

Dodsworth, W, 1814, *An historical account of the Episcopal see, and cathedral church, of Sarum, or Salisbury*

Prior, Mary, 1985, 'Reviled and crucified marriages: the position of Tudor bishops' wives', *Women in English Society 1500 – 1800*, ed Mary Prior, Methuen

Young, G M, 1939, *Portrait of an Age,* Oxford University Press reprint 1989, 87

Building the Cathedral in the 13th century: two influential women

Lady Ela, Countess of Salisbury (b Amesbury c 1187, died Lacock 1261)

Lady Ela was among the dignitaries who laid a foundation stone at the east end of the Cathedral with great ceremony in April 1220 and is described as 'one of the towering figures of the 13th century'.

She was the Countess of Salisbury in her own right but as the child of a royal ward was given by Richard I to his half-brother William Longespée, the son of Henry II and his mistress, Ida de Tosny. William assumed the title of 3rd Earl of Salisbury only by right of his marriage to Ela in 1196. Longespée's name appears in the preamble to Magna Carta as one of the great barons whose advice was sought, but was probably not present at Runnymde when the charter was sealed on 15 June 1215 because he was fighting rebels near Exeter. He and Ela had eight children and with their enormous wealth and status certainly provided financial help for the Cathedral in its early years. In 1225 Ela revealed her strength of character, refusing to remarry when it was feared that her husband had died in a shipwreck, despite pressure from the Chancellor of England who sought Ela's hand for his nephew. She was probably aware of the clause in Magna Carta that stated that 'no widow shall be compelled to marry so long as she wishes to live without a husband'. When William died the following year Ela commissioned an elaborate tomb for him in the recently completed Lady (Trinity) Chapel, leading and organising a candlelit procession from her castle at Old Sarum to his resting place. He was the first person to be buried in the Cathedral and his fine tomb with its royal *lions rampant* may today be seen in the south nave aisle.

After Longespée's death in 1226 Ela, as a rich widow, paid Henry III a vast sum to claim the high ranking position of sheriff of Wiltshire, one of only two women ever to hold that position in medieval England. Under the terms of Magna Carta

Lady Ela represented in the 1919 Peace Pageant by girls from Leehurst Convent School (© The Salisbury Museum)

only as a widow could she control her own fortune and thus contribute to 13th century political life.

She held the post of sheriff for several years before establishing two religious houses, Hinton Charterhouse for men, and her own foundation, the Augustinian nunnery at Lacock. Ela became a nun at Lacock in1237and its first Abbess two years later when the nunnery was upgraded from a priory to an abbey. She died there in 1261 and was buried in the choir of the church she founded.

Owens, Christine, 1999, 'Noblewomen and political activity', *Women in Medieval Western European Culture,* ed Linda Mitchell, Taylor and Francis

Alice Brewer and Purbeck marble

Alice was present at the consecration of the Cathedral in 1258 and her wealth and generosity were important to its early construction.

The main stone used in the building of the Cathedral is Chilmark/Tisbury Jurassic limestone, quarried just 14 miles (22 km) away but Alice Brewer from the manor of Worth Matravers gave 12 years supply of Purbeck marble. Not a genuine marble, it consists of a shelly limestone composed of fossilised densely packed sea shells, which takes a good polish. Highly prized, very expensive and difficult to work, this provided the black capitals, shafts, columns and monuments. Its contrasting impact on the interior is stunning. 12,000 tons of this prestigious 'marble' were quarried at Downshay, near Swanage, transported by ship around the coast to Christchurch and probably overland to Salisbury.

Purbeck marble is still used in the Cathedral as in the Rex Whistler memorial and more recently, the plinth of the font.

Elihonor Sadler's tomb, south nave aisle, Salisbury Cathedral
(photograph John Chandler)

Elihonor Sadler (*c*1542–1622)
The King's House

The King's House is a fine Grade I listed building, dating back to the early 13th century which now houses The Salisbury Museum. Sherborne Place, its original name, occupied a splendid site opposite the Cathedral on the West Walk, with grounds running down to the River Avon at the back. The Abbot of Sherborne lived in the Close while on duty at the Cathedral; in the 15th century the original 13th century buildings were replaced by a hall house, much of which survives as the central range of the King's House.

At the Dissolution the Benedictine monastery at Sherborne was closed, and the King's House eventually passed to the Dean and Chapter, (who still hold the freehold), and the property was leased to lay tenants. In 1564 a lease was granted to Hugh Powell of Great Durnford, a registrar to the Bishop. He made considerable alterations to the house and lived there until his death in 1587, when his widow Elihonor continued in residence. After nine years as a wealthy widow, at 53 she married the 35 year old widower Thomas Sadler, registrar to six successive bishops of Salisbury. In the late 16th and early 17th centuries, the couple made significant improvements to the house, Elihonor revealing considerable business acumen.

The Sadlers enlarged and extended the property and the magnificent brick cross-wing was added in about 1598 to the north of the 15th century range. Lit by huge mullioned windows it contained a great parlour on the ground floor, and two splendid first floor rooms with superb plaster ceilings. At the same time the adjacent abbot's chamber was enhanced, perhaps as the master bedroom. These new rooms would have provided fitting accommodation for King James I and Queen Ann of Denmark and their family who were entertained here in 1610 and 1613; James was particularly fond of Salisbury; indeed a window in the abbot's chamber has the coat of arms of his son, Henry, Prince of Wales. The change of name to the King's House commemorated these royal visits although the title was not adopted until the late 18th century.

Elizabethan brick cross wing,
The King's House, Grundy
Heape 1934

Elihonor died in 1622 at eighty, living under five monarchs and experiencing all the traumas of the Reformation. Known for her 'Pietie, Sanctitie, Charitie, and continual care of the poore' in the Close and city, her fine memorial in the south nave aisle of the Cathedral reflects the qualities of 'so good a wife and grave a matron'. Stern and devout, she is shown in life rather than in death as a diligent member of the Close community. She was buried, as requested, under her pew in the Cathedral where 'she had served God daylie almost 50 years'.

Newman, Ruth, 2010, *Living in the King's House* information pamphlet, The Salisbury Museum
Conybeare, Clare, 1987, *The King's House, Salisbury: A short history*, The Salisbury Museum
Todd, Dorothy, 1980, 'King's House in Salisbury Close', *The Hatcher Review*, Vol 1, no 9

See also 68 for The King's House

The Matrons' College
39-46 The Close

Just inside the High Street Gate (the North Gate) lies one of the more picturesque buildings of the Close, the Matrons' College of 1682-3 with major modifications in 1870. It is the only almshouse in the Close and the first charitable foundation by a Salisbury bishop since the 13th century. It was financed privately by Bishop Seth Ward (1617-1689) – an original member of the Royal Society: astronomer, scientist, mathematician, friend of Wren and Newton but also a hypochondriac with a fanatical interest in quack remedies. Possibly influenced by Christopher Wren, (although there is no evidence of this), the warm front façade of the building is brick with stone dressings with a central cupola. The arms of Charles II with a wonderful grinning lion and a Latin inscription recording the 'dedication' by Bishop Seth Ward stand above the central doorway.

Collegium hoc Matronarum
Do Co Mo
Humillime Dedicavit
Sethus Episcopus Sarum
Anno Domini
MDCLXXXII

Always for women, the College was built for ten (now eight) widows of clergymen from the dioceses of Salisbury and Exeter. Supervised by Thomas Naish, Clerk of Works at the Cathedral, the builder was Thomas Glover. In 1682 Bishop Ward entered into a contract with Glover (c.1639-1707) who agreed to remove the old buildings on the site and erect a new College at a cost of £1,193 12s 8d. Construction took only eight months and the detailed agreement between the two men survives in the Cathedral archives. Walter Pope in the late 17th century wrote of Ward's hospitality as a bachelor, a man who 'never was

View of Matrons' College through High St Gate, postcard, c1905 (© The Salisbury Museum)

destitute of Friends of the fair Sex' but he believed in celibacy and thought it 'indecent' for a bishop to marry even when he could afford to do so. However he showed his benevolence by paying for this delightful sheltered accommodation and once completed he drew up a list of statutes to cover the administration and the conduct of the matrons.

Strict rules were laid down including the following.

- The matrons had to be at least 50 years old with an income of less than £10 a year.
- Attendance at Cathedral services twice a day was compulsory, and they must behave 'soberly and respectfully towards one another' and could be fined for 'unquiet' behaviour.
- They had to remain in residence for at least eleven months each year.
- Remarriage would lead to immediate expulsion and they were forbidden to receive any stranger or other 'Persons . . . to lodge with them'.
- Apartments were to be kept 'cleane and neate'.
- Each had their own small garden and shared the use of courtyard, pump and privy and would receive six shillings pocket money every Saturday.

The rules could cause problems. In 1694 the matrons were summoned by the Dean and Chapter and strictly reminded of the conditions of residence. But this fine building probably helped rescue many widows from destitution.

Eward, Suzanne, 'Seth Ward's Widows, Early Days at the Matrons' College', 1982, *Spire,* The Fifty-Second Annual Report of the Friends of Salisbury Cathedral, 15-20
Latham Robert, 1982, *Seth Ward, Bishop of Salisbury 1667-89* (the text of an address delivered . . . in 1982 in celebration of the tercentenary of the foundation of Ward's College of Matrons), Dean and Chapter, Salisbury Cathedral

Mistress (Mary) Turberville and the 'Salisbury apparition' 17 The Close

This picturesque early 17th century Jacobean town house is comparatively unaltered. Built of brick, just two bays wide, but tall with three storeys, it has a strong simple style. The doorway is Victorian.

It was the home of Dr Daubeney Turberville (1612-1696) and his sister Mary for twenty five years in the late 17th century. He was the most famous oculist in England, treating royalty in addition to such well-known patients as Robert Boyle and Samuel Pepys. He acquired an international reputation – almost celebrity status, and is remembered in the Cathedral with a monument by the west door. **Mary** assisted her brother in his medical practice and knew his techniques and recipes. After his death she set up her own practice in London where her reputation was such that her skill was praised as an oculist in her own right.

The 'Salisbury apparition' is a well-documented 17th century ghost story. John Aubrey in 1696 recounted how a female apparition (a first wife) appeared before Mary Turberville in her 'Chamber', at No 17 The Close. The 'ghost' explained how her former husband had remarried, and her children were to be disinherited and lose their rightful legacy. She revealed that the settlement, proving her story, was hidden behind the wainscoting (panelling), by 'which means Right was done to the first Wife's children'. Further contemporary variations exist but they all agree on the hidden marriage settlement which Mistress Turberville revealed, resulting in justice.

A recent investigation by Dr John Chandler speculates on a different conclusion. He revisits all the known contemporary explanations, examines a partly obscured Cathedral floor slab to Mary Hearst, wife of William Hearst MD, (the former occupants of the house), discovers a marriage settlement in the Wiltshire and Swindon Archives and produces an alternative version for a

No 17 The Close (photograph John Chandler)

sceptical age. Chandler believes that Mary Hearst was the 'apparition' whose inheritance was threatened, surely the only known 'ghost' with a memorial in the Cathedral! After her death in 1665, with the imminent remarriage of her husband, her friends brought their concerns for Mary Hearst's son, to Mary Turberville. She was persuaded to look for the lost settlement and this was found, as in the ghost story, behind the wainscoting. So why the ghost? At a time when witchcraft and the supernatural were still widely believed, Mary Turberville, rather than embarrass William Hearst, her predecessor in the house, attributed her discovery to the apparition and then embroidered her story further with an angel and a blue mist!

Chandler, John, 2009, *The Reflection in the Pond*, Hobnob Press

See also 56 for No 17

Elizabeth Harris (1722-1781) and daughters
15 The Close, Malmesbury House

Just inside St Ann's Gate is Malmesbury House, a wonderfully elegant house with magnificent plasterwork, built on the site of a 13th century canonry. The older east part is 14th century adjoining the Close Wall. The Harris family were tenants from 1660-1850 and were responsible for extensive rebuilding in the 17th and 18th centuries including the impressive Gothick library. Visible on the outside is the attractive 1749 sundial with its quotation from *Macbeth*. The room above the gateway, St Ann's Chapel, once formed part of the house and was used for concerts in the 18th century.

James (Hermes) Harris III (1709-1780), author, philosopher and MP for Christchurch, was born and died in the city. He was the dominant figure in Salisbury's musical life and by reputation made the city 'the finest society outside London'. He was a close friend of Henry Fielding and a great admirer of Handel who visited the house in 1739. A wealthy patron of the arts, music was his passion. He married **Elizabeth Clarke** of Bridgwater in1745 and enjoyed an 'outstandingly happy marriage'. His wife, lively and intelligent, helped to make 15 The Close (later Malmesbury House) a centre of musical excellence where royalty was entertained. On one occasion, in 1762, the Duke of York, the King's brother, announced that he was to visit. The message was received at 4pm that he would be with them two hours later. But, no doubt with Elizabeth organising affairs, they managed 'a very decent supper of nineteen dishes & a very showy desert (sic) after'. 'A little musick' followed and the Duke, a violinist, 'played the whole time himself'.

Within this delightful household their two talented daughters contributed, especially Louisa (1753-1836), an accomplished musician, who unusually for a 'genteel' lady sang in private London engagements at 16 and performed with

Elizabeth Clarke of Bridgwater – Elizabeth Harris (© Hampshire Record Office, from Gertrude Robinson's day book)

professional singers. John Marsh (1752-1828), the musician and composer, lived in Salisbury from 1776 until 1783 and became part of the Harris inner circle. He described Louisa's participation in local concerts; even though she 'had a weak voice sung in a very finish'd & elegant style'.

James Harris set up annual St Cecilia concerts (which became the Salisbury Festival), in which his daughters would perform, as in 1776 when Louisa was 'inspired and sung beyond anything she ever did'. She also played the harp, the first lady to do so accompanying herself when singing.

Elizabeth Harris increasingly saw the theatre as her first love. She enjoyed the performances of Garrick in London occasionally taking Louisa and Gertrude to town with her. 'Every body', she wrote, 'is wild to see Garrick, but tis a most difficult thing to accomplish'. She was also keen on amateur dramatics, producing plays with both herself and daughter Gertrude participating, the latter increasingly taking the lead. Elizabeth said that they would act well if they can break themselves of that vile habit of laughing which at present spoils all'! Performances were for family and invited guests. They made their own sets; 'no slaves have worked harder . . . [Gertrude] was on a ladder on her knees near 12 hours.' The chapel [above St Ann's Gate] was both the music room with an orchestra and a theatre for 40-50 spectators. Everyone wanted to join the Harris girls and their troupe, even Lord Pembroke, even if only to 'snuff candles' or 'scrape on the violincello'.

Malmesbury House (photograph © Steve Stephens)

St Ann's Gate, Thomas Hearne c1790 (© The Salisbury Museum)

There appears to have been friendly rivalry between the two girls. Gertrude Harris apparently won a harpsichord in a raffle but refused to have it set up in their home because she feared that Louisa would 'prang' on it continuously. On the other hand, the sisters both found their parents' taste for 'old Handel' out of date.

One charming story has emerged when Elizabeth was horrified to see a person climbing to the top of the spire. She obtained a 'glass . . . to observe so perilous a feat', immediately dropped it, exclaiming 'Good heavens, it is James' (her son, later the first Earl of Malmesbury and leading diplomat, after whom the house is named). Her writings have a wit and vibrancy as in 1766 when at a water party, she chaperoned 'three and twenty misses' in eight boats. 'It really was very gay . . . & Harnham Bridge was crouded like Westminster Bridge at the Coronation' with everyone wanting to see them. 'Miss Wyndham had her cow most elegantly adorned & in the meadow we had sillybub.'

The above anecdotes are taken from the correspondence of this engaging family; lively first hand descriptions which provide an insight into 18th century cultural life in Salisbury Close.

Malmesbury House was let to a variety of tenants for over a century after the Harrises departed, until 1968 when it was sold by the Dean and Chapter, becoming one of few houses in the Close in private ownership at that time.

Ann Helen Marrian took over the lease in 1887. By then it seems the house did not meet the standards of comfort she expected, and she entered into a copious correspondence with the Dean and Chapter's agents to get improvements made. In 1891, for example, she wrote *I will take the house at 100£ per annum but only as a yearly tenant and with the room over the gate included ... before finally settling anything I would like to know what the Dean and Chapter will do to the house as I cannot spend another Winter here unless there is a good heating apparatus in the Hall and the fire grates are very bad. The house is very cold and I have been ill every winter . . .*

In 1913 Miss Marrian, still resident in Malmesbury House, became the first woman in Salisbury to buy a Scout motor car; 'landaulet body, painted blue with fine white lines'. Did she drive it herself, or employ a chauffeur?

Note: Scout Motors played a part in the early development of the motor trade. Vehicles were manufactured in Salisbury between 1902 and 1921. The very first car was produced in 1905, each to personal specification, reaching a peak in 1912 with over 150 men employed at the works in Bemerton. Only two Scout cars are known to survive, one of which has been bought by Salisbury Museum as an example of the city's recent industrial heritage.

The Harris archive, Hampshire Archives (ref 9M73)

Burrows, Donald, and Dunhill, Rosemary, 2002, *Music and Theatre in Handel's world: The family papers of James Harris (1732-1780),* Oxford University Press

Dunhill, Rosemary, 1997, 'Music and Drama and the Harris family of Salisbury 1735 – 1780', *The Hatcher Review,* Vol 5, no 44

Robbins, Brian (ed), 1998, *The John Marsh Journals: The Life and Times of a Gentleman Composer (1752-1828),* Pendragon Press

Correspondence between Miss Marrian and the Dean and Chapter, Wiltshire and Swindon Archives 776/982

Hicks, Ian, (ed), 2006, *Early Motor Vehicle Registration in Wiltshire 1903-1914*

Wiltshire Record Society volume 58

Charlotte Fielding, née Cradock (died 1749) 14 The Close

At the eastern end of the Close, is No 14, sometimes known as 'Fielding House' – a spacious property built in the 1660s on an older building plot. The front part of the house was refurbished in the early 18th century, including a pedimented door case surrounding the main entrance and creating the impressive, classical double fronted façade seen today. In 1899 it briefly became the vicarage for St Thomas's church.

It is associated with Henry Fielding (1707-1754), author of *Tom Jones*, described as the 'greatest comic novel in England'. There is no evidence that he actually lived in this house nor, contrary to popular opinion, that he wrote part of *Tom Jones* whilst here, but he did have strong links to Salisbury and especially to No 14.

Henry was brought up by his Grandmother, Lady Gould who won custody of the six Fielding children when Henry Fielding's father remarried a Roman Catholic. Lady Gould lived nearby in St Ann Street; Henry was able to continue his education at Eton spending his holidays in Salisbury. He was a friend of James Harris who lived at No 15 (Malmesbury House) and Harris enjoyed his company despite Fielding's huge appetite for sex, good food, snuff and drink.

In the early 1700s No 14 was occupied by Mrs Cradock, a wealthy widow with three beautiful daughters, Charlotte, Molly and Katy. They enjoyed Salisbury's social life with concerts and dances at the Assembly Rooms, probably then in New Street.

The eldest daughter, Charlotte, married Henry Fielding in 1734 bringing him a substantial dowry of £1500. He later described her as the one from whom 'I draw all the solid comfort of my life'. He was not always faithful but she eclipsed her rivals. Known for her beauty, her 'accomplished mind' and 'comfortable

No 14 The Close (photograph © Jon Stone)

dowry', they had five children and lived at the family home at East Stour. She died in 1744, probably of consumption, and was buried at St Martin in the Fields. Charlotte is preserved as the heroine of Fielding's best known novel, *Tom Jones*. Written after her death in 1749, she is clearly the model for the lively Sophia Weston.

In Fielding's last novel, *Amelia Booth*, published in 1751, he describes the hardships suffered by a young, newly married couple, Mr and Mrs Booth. His heroine Amelia is again based on his former wife. Lady Wortley Montagu later said that Fielding, in this book, gave 'a true picture of himself and Charlotte'.

Charlotte suffered an accident when she fell from a carriage and the wheel passed over her nose. This is recorded in *Amelia Booth* and in a touching section in this novel, (Book II, ch I), William Booth claimed that it was the accident which

> *made the first great impression on my heart in her favour, the injury done to her beauty by the overturning of a chaise, by which . . . her lovely nose was beat all to pieces . . . that the woman who had been so much adored for the charms of her person deserved a much higher adoration to be paid to her mind; for that she was . . . infinitely more superior to the rest of her sex.*

Later:

> About a month after the accident, when Amelia began to see company in a mask . . . I
> begged her to indulge my curiosity by showing me her face . . . (and she unmasked). The
> surgeon's skill was the least I considered . . . eagerly kissing her hand, I cried, Upon my
> soul, madam, you never appeared to me so lovely as at this instant.

Regarded possibly as a novel of atonement, this was based on Fielding's first marriage to his adored Charlotte.

Dr Edward Goldwyer, (1707-74) one of an eminent family of surgeons, lived next door at No 13 and he was the doctor who successfully operated on Charlotte's broken nose leaving her with a scar which meant that she was compelled to wear a mask for a time to cover the disfigurement as recorded in *Amelia*.

Sarah Fielding, (1710–1768), novelist

Sarah Fielding, a frequent visitor rather than a resident in the Close, has been overshadowed by her eminent older brother, Henry, but in her day, was respected and praised as a novelist. The fourth of six children, she too, after her father's second marriage, was placed in the care of Sarah Davidge Gould, her maternal grandmother, in St Ann Street Salisbury. Whilst Henry was sent to Eton, Sarah and her three sisters attended Mary Rookes's boarding school in the Close, where girls were 'to be educated and to learn to work and read and write and to talk French and Dance and be brought up as Gentlewomen'. Some of Sarah's experiences at school were later used as the basis for her novel, *The Governess; or little Female Academy* (1749). Her portrait of Mrs Teachum and her nine young pupils is certainly penned with affection. This was the earliest book written exclusively for children and to use a school setting and was much in demand when first published, and frequently imitated.

When Lady Gould died in 1733 Sarah probably left Salisbury for long periods, living at times with her sister Catharine in London, with Henry and Charlotte in Lincoln's Inn Fields, as well as in Bath and at East Stour. But her friendships from Salisbury remained important to her future writing career; Dr Arthur Collier taught her Latin and Greek; Arthur's sister, Jane became her close friend and literary collaborator. But above all, James Harris from Malmesbury House was her benefactor and gave advice on her mammoth translation from the original Greek of Xenophon's *Memoirs of Socrates* (1762). The publication was accepted as a major work of scholarship, and the pride she felt is further reinforced by the fact that it was the only book she signed with her own name.

As Henry's favourite sister, they occasionally worked together. Her first novel, by an anonymous 'lady', *The Adventures of David Simple* (1744) combined

Title page of *The Governess*, 1749, by Sarah Fielding

THE

GOVERNESS;

OR, LITTLE

FEMALE ACADEMY.

BEING

The HISTORY *of Mrs.* TEACHUM,

AND

Her NINE GIRLS.

WITH

Their NINE DAYS Amusement.

CALCULATED

For the Entertainment and Instruction of
Young LADIES in their Education.

By the AUTHOR *of* DAVID SIMPLE.

moral vision with sentimentality. For its second edition Henry added a preface, corrections and amendments 'not entirely for the good'. Sarah also published literary criticism and collections of prose, using her writing to make a modest living. Her friendship with Samuel Richardson, her brother's chief rival, meant that she moved in literary circles and enjoyed some financial patronage.

Sarah Fielding, although popular in the 18th century, remains largely unknown today although there has been a revival of interest in her work. She is increasingly viewed more sympathetically as one of the first of a class of professional female authors who succeeded in a man's world.

Battestin, M C and Probyn, C T, (eds) 1993, *The correspondence of Henry and Sarah Fielding,* Clarendon Press
Battestin, M C and Battestin, R R, 1989, *Henry Fielding: a life,* Routledge
Fielding,Henry, 1781 *Amelia,* Penguin Classics 1987

Smallpox inoculation

The Fielding, Cradock and Harris children were all involved in innovative experiments in medicine in the early 18th century, a fascinating story of upper class networking. A major outbreak of smallpox in 1723 saw over 1200 people contract the disease in the city with 165 deaths. Inoculation (using a controlled smallpox virus) had been introduced from Turkey by Lady Mary Wortley Montagu, a distant relative of Henry and Sarah Fielding.

Despite accusations that she was gambling with her own children's lives she persuaded a small group of her wealthy friends at the St Ann's Gate end of the Close, to inoculate their children and servants against smallpox. Salisbury became a pioneering centre for this method. William Goldwyre (Edward's father), of 13 The Close carried out the inoculation. The three Cradock sisters were all inoculated successfully although their servant girl 'suffered severely'.

Lady Gould arranged for the inoculation of four of her grandchildren including Henry Fielding, It appears that Sarah (14 in 1723) and her sister Ursula were not inoculated, the most obvious reason being because they had already had smallpox. The 13 year old James Harris from No 15 was also operated on with no ill effects.

This method brought huge controversy because it could spread the disease. Later, in the 1760s, the danger of infection was reduced and people were treated in their own homes. Jenner's cowpox vaccination of 1798 turned the tide.

South, Mary, 'Southampton, Salisbury and Winchester's smallpox inoculation campaigns'; *The Local Historian*, Vol 43, No2, May 2013
Grundy, Isobel, 1993, 'Inoculation in Salisbury', *The Scriblarian*, Vol 26, No 1

Dorothea Fisher (1761–1831) and daughters
The Bishop's Palace

The Bishop of Salisbury now lives in the South Canonry but the Bishop's Palace, since 1946 the location of the Cathedral School, was founded with the new Cathedral in the early 13th century. For over 700 years it was the formal home at the centre of the diocese of successive bishops, their staffs and families. But medieval bishops led itinerant lives, and so for some time there was little need to develop the building and much remains of the original structure. Bishop

Bishop's Palace, 1834, Peter Hall

Salisbury Cathedral from the Bishop's Grounds, John Constable, 1823 (© Victoria and Albert Museum)

Beauchamp, in the later 15th century, had 'made the great haulle, parler and chaumbre of the palace'. After the Restoration Seth Ward took advice from his friend Christopher Wren on rebuilding the Palace. A century later Bishop Sherlock carried out extensive refurbishment, and under Burgess (bishop 1825-37) the Palace grew to its greatest post-medieval size and remained so until the 1930s, with subsequent developments for accommodating the school.

John Fisher (1748-1825) married **Dorothea Scrivener**, an heiress from Suffolk, in 1787 and her wealth helped the couple's generous patronage of John Constable (1776-1837). The struggling artist was first invited to Salisbury in the autumn of 1811 to stay at the Palace with Bishop John Fisher and his wife. Constable was a great favourite with the highly cultured Dorothea, who thought his 'countenance is like one of the young figures in the works of Raphael'. Here he was introduced to the world of Salisbury Close which became so influential in his life.

Their daughter Dorothea (known as 'Dolly') was a skilled amateur artist, unusually in oils. On her father's instigation, she took drawing lessons from

Constable who gave her 'copying tips' and she reproduced several of his paintings. Dolly probably acted as go-between in the negotiations for one of his most famous images, *Salisbury Cathedral from the Bishop's grounds*. Commissioned by the Bishop it depicts John and Dorothea Fisher admiring 'our' Cathedral with daughter, Dolly, walking on the path towards them. Bishop Fisher, notably remarked that if only 'Constable would leave out his black clouds! Clouds are only black when it is going to rain. In fine weather the sky is blue'. A further smaller scale version of this view was commissioned by the Fishers for their younger daughter Elizabeth's wedding with 'a more serene sky'.

Wilcox, Timothy, 2011, *Constable and Salisbury, the soul of landscape,* Scala
Bailey, Anthony, 2006, *John Constable, A Kingdom of his Own,* Chatto & Windus

See also 61 for The Bishop's Palace

Maria Constable, Mary Fisher and Leadenhall

Leadenhall is so called because it was apparently the only house in the Close with a lead roofed hall. One of the original canonries of the early 13th century, it was the home of Elias of Dereham who was responsible for 25 years from 1220 for the overall construction of the Cathedral. Such was the expense of the house that Elias had to leave his successors to pay off his mortgage. The present building dates from c1720 but was reconstructed just before Archdeacon John Fisher became resident.

Leaden Hall today (2014) is an independent school for girls aged three to eleven whose mission 'is to prepare girls to become successful women of the 21st century'.

John Constable first stayed in Salisbury with Bishop John and his wife, Dorothea Fisher in 1811 and while there met his nephew, the younger John Fisher. An extraordinarily close friendship developed between the two men. Constable came to Salisbury on seven occasions between 1811 and 1829, spending his last five visits at Leadenhall with Archdeacon John (1788 -1832) and Mary Fisher.

Maria Constable (née Bicknell) (1788-1828) was the love of his life, and his art was strongly influenced by her. She visited Salisbury twice; briefly to the Bishop's Palace during their honeymoon in 1816, and for a happy seven week stay with the Fishers at Leadenhall, together with their two eldest children, in the summer of 1820. Constable had finally wed Maria after a protracted, difficult courtship lasting seven years, facing hostile opposition from her family especially her grandfather, Dr Rhudde, the rector of East Bergholt. They were very happily married for twelve years but she was never robust. She died of tuberculosis in 1828, leaving him distraught, with seven young children to bring up. But in 1820, at Leadenhall, he was in a buoyant, productive mood, inspired by Maria, and his paintings are full of life, whether of the Cathedral, the river Avon or the meadows. These changed after her death as he became more melancholy and inward looking.

Portrait of Maria Bicknell, dated 10 July 1816, a few months before her marriage on 2 October 1816. John Constable wrote telling her that 'I would not be without your portrait . . . [it] calms my spirits . . . and it is always the first thing I see in the morning and the last thing at night'. Constable was not a successful portrait painter but this is a wonderfully intimate, tender picture, where his love for Maria shines through.
Maria Bicknell, Mrs John Constable, John Constable, 1816 (NO2655 © Tate, London 2014)

This portrait of Mary Fisher shows great care and delicacy towards his subject. She is shown with ringlets, a fashionably low cut dress, pearl necklace and a pendant crucifix. It was painted in 1816 during the Constables' honeymoon at Osmington on the Dorset coast, with John and Mary Fisher, who had also recently married.
Mrs Mary Fisher, John Constable, 1816 (© the Fitzwilliam Museum, Cambridge)

Mary Fisher (c 1791-1856) was the daughter of Dr William Cookson, a canon of St George's Chapel, Windsor. She was the cousin of the poet, William Wordsworth, whose radical 'French principles' caused some consternation to the conservative Cookson and Fisher families! The archdeacon described his wife

Leadenhall, Elizabeth Wickens, 1832 (© Wiltshire Museum, Devizes)

as 'quiet & silent & sits & reads without disturbing a soul' but Mary provided loyal support and friendship, both to Maria and to John Constable after his wife's death. The artist told Mary sometime later that he felt Maria's presence and still lived 'in the society of my departed Angel'. During Constable's last two visits to Salisbury in 1829, he came with his children, John Charles and Minna. The warmth of the Fisher household and his love for the Close helped to revive him, and his daughter happily prolonged her stay enjoying the company of the six Fisher children after her father had returned to London. Mary ensured that Minna's education was not neglected even sending her to the law courts to hear trials. The Fishers encouraged the grieving artist to undertake, in the same year, perhaps his greatest iconic work, 'Salisbury Cathedral from the Meadows'.

Wilcox, Timothy, 2011, *Constable and Salisbury, the soul of landscape,* Scala
Bailey, Anthony, 2006, *John Constable, A Kingdom of his Own,* Chatto & Windus

Harnham Gate

Harnham Gate is contemporary with the Close Wall dating from the mid-14th century and is still locked every night. The more rural southern end of the Close, with its smaller houses, is in dramatic contrast to the grandeur of the stately homes along the West Walk. Its special quality was captured in a painting by John Constable in 1821.

The following account gives a vivid picture of this humble, domestic area in the early 19th century. Taken from William Small's memoirs (1881) he recalls that Mrs Truckle, described as a hawker in a contemporary account, used to live in one of the houses by the gate. Small writes of how she 'used to travel the country with Haberdashery . . . she had a grey poney & trap. The poney used to feed in the Close by the side of the Road . . . Mrs Woodyear & her daughter Martha lived in the Corner house under a stately Elm tree . . . long since cut down. She used to keep a nightingale in a Cage. Outside her front Door'. (Punctuation and spelling as in original text.)

Harnham Gate, postcard, *c* 1905 (© The Salisbury Museum)

The illustration shows a busy but tranquil scene at the southern end of the Close in the aftermath of war in 1945. Photograph 1945 (© Wiltshire and Swindon Archives, G23/998/1)

Note: William Small (1820–1890) wrote his memoirs in 1881. He described his childhood, family and acquaintances, and his work as a craftsman in the city. He was employed on several well known buildings in Salisbury including The King's House, 19 The Close and Mompesson House. Such working class memories are extremely rare and give a fresh insight into 19th century life in Salisbury. A transcription, with extensive introduction, has been published by the Wiltshire Record Society, see 'further reading'.

Wilts and Dorset Female Penitentiary 1831-1851 De Vaux House

The Female Penitentiary stood on the site of De Vaux House, within the Liberty of the Close, but just outside the Harnham Gate. A rough flint wall and buttress are remaining fragments of De Vaux College, a fledgling medieval university established for 'poor, needy, honourable and teachable scholars', which

De Vaux lodge 2014, (photograph Joe Newman)

attracted Oxford students from the 13th century to the 16th century. The arms of Oxford University are displayed on the house.

Founded in 1831, the Wilts Female Penitentiary Association set out to establish 'an asylum to that unhappy class of our fellow creatures whose melancholy situation necessarily renders them outcasts of society'. This institution was an early example of a refuge for rescuing fallen women off the streets, to give them an opportunity to reform their lives by training them for menial work in domestic service. The origins of this movement can be traced to the mid 18th century, and by the late 1840s there were eight such establishments in London, and 13 elsewhere in England. The best known run by the Church of England were the House of Mercy at Clewer near Windsor (1849), the House of Peace in Plymouth (1850), and the House of Mercy at Bussage (1851). Among the Salisbury founders were the Bishop, Thomas Burgess, and the Dowager Countess of Pembroke (who subsequently bequeathed a legacy of £500 to the Penitentiary and £1,000 to the Infirmary, in 1856). The governing body continued to represent the authorities of the diocese and there was always a 'ladies committee' concerned with fund-raising and with over-seeing (at a suitable distance) the welfare of the inmates.

The first two girls admitted in October 1831 were Anne Mould aged 17 and Mary Ann Beale aged 15; both left to go into service in February 1834. At the time of the 1851 census there were nine 'penitents', two from Devon and Middlesex and the others from around Wiltshire. The matron was Elizabeth Lewis from Shaftesbury, and her assistant was a Canadian by birth.

Over the years, inmates came from throughout the Salisbury Diocese, and much further afield, including Bristol, Birmingham and the Channel Islands. They varied widely in age, and in the length of time they stayed. Not all the women benefited from the regime: reasons for departure included 'was very disorderly', 'sent to Weymouth Union on account of ill-health', and 'found to be pregnant and sent to her parish'.

However, the annual report of 1850 looked back over the previous decade with some satisfaction, and commented that 79 females had been admitted to the institution '... many of these having been redeemed from a life of sin and wretchedness are now fulfilling respectable stations in society as wives, mothers or domestic servants'.

Not long after this the institution moved away from the Close. Funds were 'applied in purchasing certain buildings and premises in St Martin's Church Street, Salisbury, extending back to the Meadows, this affording an eligible spot for the healthy recreation of the inmates'. This was the former location of Salisbury's Roman Catholic congregation, for whom in 1848 a new Roman Catholic church had been opened in Exeter Street. The penitentiary renamed it St Martins Home.

Later in the 19th century it became the Diocesan House of Mercy, then St Mary's Home, run by religious sisters from Clewer. Its operation increased in scale, including a large commercial laundry, and it did not finally close until the 1950s.

Archives of penitentiary, Wiltshire and Swindon Archives D401
Elliott, J, 2003, ''Saved to Serve': fallen women in Salisbury', *Sarum Chronicle 3*
Prochaska, F, 1980, *Women and Philanthropy in 19th century England*, Clarendon Press
Salisbury Journal 26 Dec 1831

The Miss Wyndhams
19 The Close (Sarum College)

Number 19 The Close was built from 1677 for Francis Hill, a distinguished London lawyer and Deputy Recorder of Salisbury, on the site of two earlier tenements. A house of elegance, the front door faced the Bishop's Walk and the palace where Bishop Seth Ward had just completed work on the great hall. Perhaps Hill saw some sense of equality between himself and the Bishop, suggesting that the church and the law were the two great pillars of 17th century English society. Members of the extensive Wyndham family owned No 19 from 1768 to1797 and again from 1828 to 1859. In 1828 an advertisement described the house as having a *handsome entrance hall, two sitting rooms, dining and breakfast, with housekeeper's room, butler's pantry, store-room and an excellent kitchen, with large cellars. The second floor contains a handsome drawing room and three best bedrooms, besides a smaller one for a servant and seven rooms in the attic.* Behind the house were coach-house, stables and brewhouse. All this for two middle aged ladies, known as the Miss Wyndhams of the Close.

The following extract is taken from '*Cherished Memories and Associations*' by William Small (1820-1890), painter and glazier, and gives an insight into two former residents ignored in conventional histories. Henrietta (1777-1860) and Charlotte (1779-1859) were the unmarried daughters of William Wyndham and Elizabeth Heathcote of Dinton. Charlotte bought the lease of No19 in 1828. By 1851, Henrietta (74) is described as the 'head' with sister Charlotte (72), living there as 'fundholders' with two female domestic servants and a footman.

William Small has some sympathetic details of '*these two excellent ladies*', including their fear of thunderstorms!

We had the pleasure of working for [them] *until their death, a period of about 20 years . . . their house is now standing,* [1881] *and used as the Theological College. Miss Henrietta was the Mistress of the Establishment, & gave all orders, Miss Charlotte was a nice lady, but very reserved and was seldom seen. It was a good house . . . allways* (sic)

Sarum College, 2011 (photograph Sue Johnson)

plenty of Home Brew'd beer & Bread & Meat often, Miss Henrietta had an excellent taste for Matching Colours, & knew all the tints that composed them . . . She would often say to us, when we left at 6 Oclock, Now come at 8 & have some supper with my servants, & it was the best of everything. I was there one afternoon in July, & there was a very severe storm of thunder & lightning, they both came into the bed room where I was at work, they were much alarmed . . . & so Miss Charlotte, went into a dark ward robe & shut the door. & Miss Henrietta went behind the bed curtain's (sic) *close to the wall, until the storm was abated. They were very charitable to the poor & gave a great many Christmas Boxes.* [Punctuation and spelling as in original text.]

There is a memorial to both Charlotte and Henrietta in Dinton Church.

The lease of the house was acquired in 1860, the year after Charlotte's death, by Bishop Kerr Hamilton for the sum of £1700 to found the Theological College, while William Butterfield's contrasting Victorian gothic extension (on the right), including the flint and stone chapel was completed in 1881. The college closed in 1994 becoming the ecumenical study and research centre, Sarum College.

Frances Child (*c*1787–1869)
52 The Close

One of the more fanciful descriptions we have of the Close in the 19th century comes from the pen of Miss Child. Frances Child was born in Romsey, and seems to have lived in the Close most of her adult life. Her home was at No 52 (now the offices of Friends of the Cathedral) from where she had an excellent view of the comings and goings through the High Street Gate, and people passing around Choristers' Green. The buildings, opposite Matrons' College, fronting the road between the High Street Gate and the corner of the Green were 15th century cottages and shops. The two shops that became No 52, after alterations over time, were occupied by lay vicars in the 17th century, and from 1800 had non-clerical tenants.

Miss Child wrote in sing-song – some might say painful – rhyming couplets about many significant events in the city, such as the Exhibition of 1852 and the peace celebrations of 1856, but 'The Spinster at Home in the Close' (1844) is probably the best known. In it she not only described her house

A tiny abode, well befitting a Spinster
In a nook of the Close, which belongs to its Minster
I can look from my window and see the west end
Of that glorious pile which we all must commend

But also related her day to day life

I have friends, too, who frequently ask me to dine
When I taste of choice viands and sip the best wine

As Edith Olivier put it unsympathetically she also 'collected the legends and traditions of Salisbury and its cathedral in the spirit of an un-critical and simple-minded old gossip, and this is indeed what she was'. In the 1851 census Miss Child described herself as 'fundholder & author in subjects of topography'.

THE

SPINSTER AT HOME,

IN THE

CLOSE OF SALISBURY.

———

NO FABLE.

———

TOGETHER WITH

TALES AND BALLADS.

———

BY

MISS CHILD.

———

" I 've often wish'd that I could write a book,
Such as all English people might peruse :
I never should regret the pains it took—
That 's just the sort of fame that I should choose."

FRERE.

———

SALISBURY:
W. B. BRODIE AND CO.
LONDON : HATCHARD AND SON, PICCADILLY ; SIMPKIN AND MARSHALL,
STATIONERS'-HALL-COURT.
———
M.DCCC.XLIV.

Title page of *A Spinster at Home in the Close of Salisbury*

Although she must have read widely, and collected copious notes for her poem, it is difficult to confirm much of what is claimed as historical fact. A recent attempt by Steve Hobbs and Sue Johnson, published in *Sarum Chronicle,* to pursue part of what she had written as 'An Historical Appendix' published in 1852 decided that it was not possible to establish authenticity without reasonable doubt. That need not detract from the pleasure Frances Child obviously took in her life, and the value we gain from the atmosphere she creates, and what she did achieve was to preserve some old Salisbury stories which might otherwise have been forgotten.

Hobbs, S, and Johnson, S, 2004, 'The Spinster and the Plague', *Sarum Chronicle* 4,

Elizabeth Wickens (*c*1788–1866)
25 The Close

No 25 is in Rosemary Lane, and lies across the backs of No 26 and No 27. The house today is largely as Miss Wickens would have known it, and dates to the early 18th century when redevelopment was made to a much older structure. Two separate tenements were combined in the mid – 17th century, and the rooms from that time can still be identified. No 25 was the first home of the Godolphin School from 1784 to 1788.

Elizabeth Wickens was one of several members of the Wickens family who lived in this house. She was an independent lady ('fundholder' in the 1851 census) who had gained a reputation as an amateur artist, sufficiently skilled and confident to submit work to the Royal Academy. Specialising in local topographical and antiquarian features, one of her projects was to record 'Remains of Antiquity in the City of Salisbury. All Drawn on the Spot'.

Miss Wickens is particularly remembered for drawing the doom painting in St Thomas's church after it was initially uncovered in 1819, following centuries under whitewash. Her sketch was subsequently engraved and published in Hatcher's *History of Salisbury* (1843).

In the Salisbury 1852 exhibition she entered a collection that included 'Two drawings of the Fair anciently held in the Close at Whitsuntide' and a 'Drawing of the Nave of Sarum Cathedral'. Two years later, when Mary Nichols accompanied her father to the annual meeting of the Wiltshire Archaeological & Natural History Society held in Salisbury she wrote in her diary 'I amused myself by looking over a book of drawings of various Antiquities in Salisbury by Miss Wickens, a lady of antiquarian taste long resident in the city'.

When she died in 1866 Elizabeth Wickens left bequests to the Society for Assisting the Poor Clergy of Wilts, the Matrons College and Salisbury Infirmary, as well as numerous legacies 'in connection with the Cathedral'. The latter included money for restoration work, books for the Library, and the interest on £500 'to encourage the study and practice of Protestant sacred music from selections of Green, Gibbons, Purcell, Jeremiah Clarke, and Croft'.

Picture of North Walk, No 25 is on the far right hand side, No 26 is the creeper-covered house next to it, and No 27 is the small house in the centre. Thomas Sharp, 1949, *Newer Sarum, a plan for Salisbury* (© Salisbury City Council)

More lady artists

Several notable amateur artists feature in this book. Painting and drawing, along with music and decorative needlework, were skills learned by leisured women and considered appropriate ways of deploying their time. Relatively few received any notice beyond their own family, but in the 19th century, as in the case of Elizabeth Wickens, there were increasing opportunities such as exhibitions and bazaars when their output was revealed to the public.

Nearly 50 years after Salisbury's 1852 event, there were a series of 'Exhibitions of Pictures' held at Church House, Crane Street, in which several ladies of the Close played a prominent part. **Miss Hussey of the Wardrobe**, **Miss Jacob of Myles Place** and **Miss Townsend of Mompesson House** were all members of the organising committees in 1897, 1898 and 1899. Several hundred items were put on display, and complimentary comments made in the newspaper reports of these occasions: 'displaying considerable skill', 'a clever sketch', and 'a noticeable contribution' for example.

Margaret Hussey died in 1941, aged 90. She was one of four sisters who were all born at the Wardrobe in the Close. They 'were fond of painting, and Miss

Margaret was also accomplished in other arts. It was as a musician perhaps that she was best known'. She was one of the first and most enthusiastic members of the Salisbury Musical Society, where she played the cello in the orchestra for 16 years. 'Miss Hussey excelled at wood-carving' and was 'an artistic needlewoman'. Her obituary thus epitomised the qualities expected of an upper-middle class woman who had been brought up in the Victorian period.

Thanks to Sue Johnson

Salisbury 1852 exhibition catalogue
Mary Nicols Travel Diary X, Surrey History Centre
Salisbury Journal 25 September 1897, 1 October 1898, 23 September 1899
Salisbury Times 17 January 1941
Chandler, John, 2012, 'The Damned Bishop', *Sarum Chronicle* 12

Henrietta Lear (1824 –1896)
17 The Close

In 1859 Henrietta Louisa Farrer married Rev Sidney Henry Lear, the second son of the Dean of Salisbury, and chaplain to Bishop Hamilton. Most of their short married life was spent abroad on account of her husband's health. Only eight years later Henrietta was widowed, and then lived at No 17 the Close until she died in 1896 at the age of 73.

Henrietta Lear was a prolific author on religious topics. Her diverse publications included 'books of devotion' that went into numerous editions, biographical sketches of persons 'of saintly character', translations, works for children, and collections of prose and verse. *A Lenten Cookery Book, being nearly 200 Maigre recipes* is still in print. It includes instructions for Salisbury Buttered Eggs.

Her life was not entirely committed to penning large quantities of serious and sacred words. In memory of her husband Mrs Lear donated £1,000 to pay for a splendid new chancel screen in brass and iron for the Cathedral, by Skidmore of Coventry. She was a strong supporter of the Salisbury Theological College, and contributed to their funds also, especially for the chapel. Her generosity was appreciated by many charitable causes in the area.

Towards the end of her life Mrs Lear *planned and carried out a scheme for having a room* [in Gigant Street] *open every evening, where games and books should be provided, smoking allowed, and where warmth and brightness should attract even passing labourers or tramps to turn in and spend the evening, instead of at a public house.*

An anonymous 'brief memoir' of Henrietta Lear provides a striking description

119.—Salisbury Buttered Eggs.

Hard-boil and chop the eggs, put into a stew-pan with butter, and season with pepper ; mix well with a raw egg to blend. Serve on hot toast, and brown over with crumbs.

Henrietta Lear's recipe for Salisbury buttered eggs from *A Lenten Cookery Book* 1876

The Skidmore screen in the Cathedral from Truby 1948 *The Glories of Salisbury Cathedral*

of her days at their most busy: *she habitually rose at 4.30 or 5, and spent an hour or two in prayer and meditation until it was time to go to the 7.30 cathedral Matins ... From 8 to 9 am she devoted to letter-writing, and would dash off 8 or 9 letters often long ones before her nine o'clock breakfast. After that a couple of hours in the district* [visiting the sick and poor, probably for St Martin's parish]*, and an hour or so at her big embroidery frame* [she made several altar frontals for the Cathedral] *... would complete her morning. And the afternoon would be given to her guests, and to social duties and pleasures, with Evensong at the cathedral; and then literary writing of some kind till dinner, and again till bedtime if alone, and if not she would frequently write on after her guests had gone to their rooms.*

After a heart attack Henrietta Lear led a much quieter life. Her long-serving domestic staff not only cared for her but also enabled her to continue her philanthropic work: 'sick and infirm people were visited, books were lent, and comforts provided'. At her death, it was said 'many will feel that they have lost a true and generous friend'.

Henrietta Lear's sister-in-law was the second wife of Thomas Gambier Parry, mother of Sidney Gambier Parry (see under Jane Weigall), and step-mother of composer Hubert Parry. The latter, then a young man of 23, was staying with Henrietta at the time of the 1871 census; he was described as her nephew, and Mus. Bac. Oxon. Parry had been the youngest ever candidate to pass the Oxford Bachelor of Music degree exam in 1866. Perhaps he was staying with his 'aunt' to be near, but not too close, to Lady Maude Herbert with whom he had fallen in love, against the wishes of both parents. They became clandestinely engaged in 1870, and were married in June 1872 after Parry had embarked on a career as a Lloyds underwriter.

The benefaction of the Skidmore screen is surprisingly frequently attributed to Dean Francis Lear's widow, even in otherwise apparently authoritative accounts of the furnishings of Salisbury Cathedral. How this error came about is not clear, though the family interconnections are complex. Francis Lear was Dean from 1846-1850. Among his children were Francis who held a number of offices in the Cathedral, Sidney who married Henrietta, Isabel who was the wife of Bishop Walter Kerr Hamilton, and Ethelinda who became the second wife of Thomas Gambier Parry. In Henrietta Lear's obituaries, and the anonymous memoir of her written shortly after her death, it is stated that she was the donor in memory of her husband Sidney. This is correctly confirmed in *some* other volumes on the Cathedral (for example Gleeson White's *The Cathedral Church of Salisbury,* 1898).

St Martin's *Parish Magazine* Dec 1896
Mrs H L Sidney Lear, 1897, *'Joy': a fragment,* to which is prefixed a brief memoir of the author
Salisbury Journal 4 November 1876; 14 November 1896

Jane Weigall (1838–1906)
9 The Close

The relationship between the houses on the corner of Bishops Walk and North Walk, Nos 8 and 9 and their predecessor buildings, is complex, and changed over time. A new house seems to have been built in the 1660s, and separate leases were issued for the two parts from about 1700. No 9 has a beautiful Tuscan porch with domed hood while the Georgian exterior masks the earlier structure. It was the first home of the Diocesan Training College, before it moved to No 11

Jane Weigall's memorial plaque in the Cathedral (photograph Peter Liversage)

Te Deum altar frontal embroidered by Jane Weigall and her daughter (courtesy of Salisbury Cathedral © Ash Mills)

and then to the Kings House. Jane and Alfred Weigall later lived at No 9. A brass memorial plaque to Jane Weigall in the north choir aisle of the Cathedral erected by 'her grateful children' gives her dates, and states simply that she was 'for nearly forty years a daily worshipper in this Cathedral'.

Jane was a sister of W S Gilbert, of Gilbert & Sullivan fame. In 1857 she married Alfred Weigall, a professional artist known particularly for miniatures. They had ten children.

The obituary published in the *Salisbury Journal* July 1906 adds to this: 'she devoted a great deal of her time to Church needlework and … had worked two handsome altar frontals for the Cathedral … at the time of her death she was working on another.' These are known to be 'Te Deum' and 'The Evangelists' both designed by Sidney Gambier Parry, and it is thought 'Annunciation' is the third. Her daughter Edith Aldworth shared this skill and enthusiasm.

Parry was an architect, half-brother to the composer Hubert Parry. As well as designing these splendid frontals, he had another local connection as his maternal grandfather was Dean Francis Lear.

Jane Weigall was involved in other philanthropic voluntary work in the area. She was a regular 'visitor' to the workhouse, for example providing tea and entertainment to the inmates of the Workhouse Infirmary in 1880, and donating a pall for use at funerals in 1895. Her husband Alfred Weigall was a long-serving Poor Law Guardian.

Although not immediately obvious, Mrs Weigall was a resident of the Close who took a number of different active roles in the community.

See also Henrietta Lear

Poor Law Guardians archives, Wiltshire and Swindon Archives H1/110
Salisbury Journal 28 July 1906

Annie Moberly (1846-1937)
The Bishop's Palace

George Moberly was Bishop of Salisbury from 1869 to his death in 1885. Mrs Mary Ann Moberly ran a huge household (with at least a dozen servants) and Edith Olivier comments *there were a great many parties at the palace, all carefully planned and thought out. Enormous parties for diocesan conferences when clergy from remote villages met … Learned parties for translators of the Bible; musical parties for friends of the brothers; friendly parties for a few intimates from the Close, and family parties for all ages.*

One of their fifteen children, Charlotte Anne Elizabeth (always known as Annie) acted as her father's secretary and then nurse/companion until she was almost 40. Her own education had begun at home with her mother and a governess, and she shared some of her brothers' lessons. The family's close association with Rev John Keble and with author Charlotte M Yonge influenced their thinking and outlook on life. Annie developed her knowledge through reading in her father's library, and by her contact with the many visitors to the palace.

After Bishop Moberly's death Mrs Moberly and her three remaining unmarried daughters, Alice, Edith and Annie, moved out of the Palace and into The Hall in New Street. Before long Annie was invited by Elizabeth Wordsworth, the sister of the new bishop and principal of Lady Margaret Hall, to move to Oxford and take charge of a new Anglican hall for women students. St Hugh's Hall opened in 1886 with four students in a north Oxford semi-detached house. Renamed St Hugh's College in 1911, at the time of Annie Moberly's retirement in 1915 there were 60 students and a staff of tutors.

Annie Moberly's impeccable credentials earned the confidence of parents who might otherwise have had doubts about their daughters pursuing higher education. Students were expected to work hard, to develop a sense of community. Sport, music and sociability were encouraged.

Annie Moberly, from *Four Victorian Ladies of Wiltshire*, 1945, Edith Olivier

The seventh daughter of a seventh child, Annie Moberly acknowledged she heard voices, saw apparitions and experienced time travel, although she kept this firmly within the boundaries of her strict faith. Visiting Versailles in 1901 with her friend Eleanor Jourdain (Vice-Principal of St Hugh's from 1902), they believed they met Marie Antoinette and wrote about it in a famous ghost story '*An Adventure*'. There is a long-held tradition in Salisbury of 'The Bishop's Birds' – large white birds fly overhead on the death of a bishop. Annie Moberly did indeed record that she saw them while walking in the Palace grounds a few hours after her father died.

Keene, A, 2003, 'Mother of the House', *Oxford Today: the University Magazine*, Vol 15 No 2
Moberly, C A E, 1911, *Dulce Domum*, John Murray
Smith, Peter L, 2013, *The Bishop's Palace at Salisbury*, Spire Books

See also 84 for Dora Robertson
See also 37 for The Bishop's Palace

Maria Fawcett (1830-1923)
27 The Close

No 27 is a small house of only two storeys that stands out as surprisingly low in the row of buildings on North Walk. Belonging to the vicars choral, it was sublet and became neglected until leased and renovated by John Peniston in the second decade of the 19th century. An advertisement for a tenant in 1836 described it as 'genteel, consisting of drawing and dining rooms, small parlour, kitchen and offices, four best bedrooms and servants' attics'.

William Fawcett was mayor of Salisbury at the time of the 1832 Reform Act. He and his wife Mary moved to the Close in the 1860s. They had three sons and a daughter. Sarah Maria Fawcett lived here at No 27 with her parents until their deaths in old age in the 1880s, and then alone for another 34 years. Her younger brother Henry was the blind Postmaster-General in Gladstone's second ministry, and so her sister-in-law was Millicent Garrett Fawcett (they were visiting Salisbury at the time of both the 1871 and 1881 censuses).

One year of Maria's diary survives – for 1895 – which she wrote in Italian during the week and French on Saturdays and Sundays. The short factual entries reveal the breadth of her interests and activities. She was a school governor (at the Godolphin School 1885-1914), secretary for girls of the Oxford and Cambridge Local Examinations; she attended lectures, concerts, bazaars, sports; she read, wrote letters, paid visits, went for drives and walks, holidayed in London and the Isle of Wight.

Maria and Millicent had always got on well: Millicent wrote

I received a most generous and loving welcome into this home circle, and I cannot speak with sufficient reverence and gratitude of my sister-in-law Maria Fawcett. From the time of the accident [when HF lost his sight 1858] until our marriage she had been all in all to her brother, lavishing on him her great love and watchful care: now, when I appeared suddenly, to her, upon

Maria Fawcett (courtesy of
Godolphin School)

*the scene, she did not look upon me as a supplanter, but welcomed me as a
comrade and friend. I have never known a nobler or more generous nature.
She was so full of loving appreciation, there was no room in her heart for
jealousy or suspicion.*

Millicent visited Salisbury when Maria was ill in March 1895

Friday 8th	Millicent visited me in the afternoon
Sat	I felt better. Millicent visited Eliza [recently widowed sister-in-law] after tea
Sun	I felt better but I still stayed in bed. Millicent read to me 'the Life of the Queen' which she had written [pub 1895].
Mon	It was fine weather. Millicent and Miss Cohen went walking after lunch.
Tuesday	Maria returned to London. Her visit was enjoyable

Fawcett, M G, 1924, *What I Remember,* T Fisher Unwin
Sarah Maria Fawcett's diary 1895 Wiltshire and Swindon Archives acc 2954
Salisbury Journal 31 October 1836

Barbara Townsend (1842–1939)
Mompesson House

Mompesson House, built in 1701, on the site of older properties, is one of the finest houses in the Close. Sir Thomas Mompesson MP for New Sarum died in 1701and his son Charles lived in the house until his own death in 1714. Subsequent tenants were members of the Longueville and Portman families, until the Townsends lived there from the 1840s to 1939. Mompesson House was the residence of the Bishop from 1946 to 1951, and in 1952 it was bought by Denis Martineau who gave it to the National Trust. They took over on his death in the 1970s, and opened it to the public, decorated and furnished in keeping with its 18th century architecture.

Photograph of Barbara Townsend in old age (courtesy of the late Mark Walford)

Mompesson House by George Henton 1888, watercolour, at Mompesson House, Salisbury, Wiltshire, (22685 © National Trust Images)

Externally the house remains much as it was when rebuilt in 1701, including Charles Mompesson's monogram in the iron gates. About 1740 the magnificent plasterwork and new chimney-pieces and overmantels were added. William Small described how his family firm painted 'the greater portion of the inside' for Mr Townsend in 1850. 'The elegant Entrance Hall, Stair Case & Landings we grained, dark Oak Cob & varnished, which had a very rich & grand effect. The elegant Panell'd walls of the Stair Case, with their beautiful plaster work, were painted pea green & picked out in a rich cream colour'.

The Townsends were one of the professional upper-middle class families living in the Close in Victorian times. George Barnard Townsend was a solicitor specialising in railway land acquisition, he took on the lease of Mompesson House in 1846. A cricketer and yachtsman, he also had property in Mudeford on the south coast. Mr Townsend married his next-door neighbour from the Hungerford Chantry Elizabeth Eyre. They had a son George, and three daughters Barbara, Jane and Gertrude. On Elizabeth's death a few years later a door was made between the two properties and the children treated both houses as their home. In the 1851 census Barbara was given the status of 'visitor' at the Hungerford Chantry. Jane sadly died young and her widower and three young children moved back to Mompesson House; her daughters too were widowed, and returned to live with 'Auntie Bar' and 'Auntie Ger'.

Barbara never married, but took part in all the typical female activities of provincial society at the time, and watched over her sister's children. Her particular interest and skill was in sketching and painting, and her charming delicate works have been described as 'in the style of a Japanese Renoir'. She was a familiar figure about the Close in a large hat, copious shawls and veils, and her art equipment. Not only did she create many watercolours of the Close and its inhabitants, but she described it in delightful detail: 'it required two hands, two feet and all the body skilfully aligned before it was possible, in a crinoline, to pass modestly through the little white wooden posts placed close together at the entrance to the Cathedral green.' Towards the end of the 1930s Mompesson House was said to be 'crowded with the harvest of Barbara's long life'.

National Trust, *Mompesson House guide book* 2008
Personal communication

Diocesan Training College
at The King's House

From 1851, the King's House became home to the Diocesan Training College for female students, later (from 1965 to 1978) the College of Sarum St Michael. This was one of the first teacher training colleges for women in Britain, originally opened in No 9 The Close under the formidable Mrs Margaret Duncan, who had been appointed as Superindendent and Lady Governess. When she retired in 1862 more than 500 women had qualified as elementary schoolmistresses under her care. One of them recalled that she was 'beloved by the young people to

The King's House c1805, John Buckler (© The Salisbury Museum)

Diocesan Training College students with their bicycles c1900 (© The Salisbury Museum)

whom she was very kind, but very strict in requiring attention to every one of her rules and regulations'.

The students' regime was indeed rigorous, with emphasis on a strong Christian tradition. Teaching practice was offered initially in the Model School attached to the college, but real 'hands-on' experience was quickly made available in the city schools, with St Edmund's Girls' School providing a retiring room where students could 'recover their nerves'.

Thomas Hardy's two sisters, Mary and Katherine, were students here. When admitted in 1860 Mary's 'state of acquirement' was described as 'backward' but her progress record showed a 'diligent' and 'very willing' student.

Kate (Katherine) arrived in 1877 with the advantage of having been a pupil teacher in Dorset, but her experiences of the authoritarian discipline provided Hardy with the first-hand material on which to base Sue Bridehead's encounters at the college in 'Melchester' in *Jude the Obscure* (published 1895). Desperately unhappy, Sue's escape by fording the river at the back of the college was clearly inspired by an intimate knowledge of the buildings.

By 1900 with a new chapel (currently 2014, the lecture hall of the Museum), further dormitories, and the luxuries of electric lighting and heating, there were some 100 students. During World War I their personal freedom was seriously restricted. They were initially banned from the main streets, since it was believed that soldiers 'had brought disease' into the city. By 1915 however expeditions on bicycles were permitted for botany classes, and students attended plays and concerts at the Assembly Rooms, on the corner of New Canal and the High Street.

But the trend for larger, secular higher education institutions meant that by the 1970s the College was no longer viable, and it finally closed in 1978.

Most of the more modern buildings were converted into apartments that house a wide variety of residents, many of them women, seeking a peaceful place to live, between the imposing beauty of the Cathedral itself and the tranquillity of the river. Some are retired, and 'leisured' in the sense that Edith Olivier used the adjective, having the freedom to choose how to use their time and make their activities contribute to the community in many ways. Susan Howatch (b 1940) the author, writes that 'The Cathedral and the Close form a small enclosed world, ideal for a novelist to re-create, explore and examine'. She bought two flats at Sarum St Michael in the 1980s, 'one for living in and one for working'. Here she wrote her 'Starbridge' novels, based on Salisbury, covering the spiritual and domestic experiences of Anglican clergymen and their families from the 1930s to the 1960s.

Be they authors or artists, philanthropists or entrepreneurs, they all appreciate the 'most congenial atmosphere' of Salisbury Close.

Head, Jenny and Johns, Anne, *Inspired to Teach* (publication date April 2015)
Taylor, Lucy, 1988, *College in the Close: Sarum St Michael 1841-1978*

See also 19 for King's House

Girls at Bishop Wordsworth's School, 11 The Close

Much of No 11 was rebuilt in the mid 18th century and the house now forms part of Bishop Wordsworth's School. The front façade is in red brick with stone dressings but the side walls are faced with mathematical tiles, possibly the earliest example of many in Salisbury. (Mathematical tiles were a Georgian invention, designed to deceive the observer and appear as high quality brickwork). The building also housed the Diocesan Training College which moved here from

Girls on the tennis courts, with pet goats, 1905 (courtesy of Bishop Wordsworth's School)

Girls at Bishop Wordsworth's School 1905 (courtesy of Bishop Wordsworth's School)

No 9 remaining until 1850. In 1846 'a pretty little ceremony took place' and the pupils presented 'their Instructress, Mrs Duncan with a very elegant copy of the holy scriptures, as a token of their regard'.

Bishop Wordsworth's School was founded in 1890 by the progressive cleric, John Wordsworth (1843-1911), the great-nephew of the poet William Wordsworth. Bishop of Salisbury from 1885 until his death, he was an academic, passionate to promote Anglican schools in the city and particularly keen to establish a boys' secondary school. In January 1890 the school opened for 45 boys in the Bishop's Palace, moving into purpose built accommodation some months later on the present site. The boys initially paid 9d a week.

In 1902 girls were admitted and, following the Education Act of that year, it became a secondary co-ed grammar school. Margaret Richards, the daughter of the first headmaster Reuben Bracher and one of the early students, wrote of her time here. Starting in 1908, she went on to win a scholarship to Bristol University. For much of the time the boys and girls were kept separate, both in classes and playgrounds. There were iron gates between the two playgrounds intended to be kept locked, and boys were often caned if they strayed into the 'wrong' playground. The girls went to science labs and classrooms at the Art School, 49-51 New Street, but in the post war period they moved on to the Close site and occupied two ground floor schoolrooms, also keeping 'neat gardens'. Sixth form groups were mixed in at least some subjects.

Sports Day was a great event for the boys; the 'envious girls in their white frocks and hard hats could do little else but watch' but they did play tennis and netball on the school playgrounds.

They took part in the 1919 Peace pageant for all the schools in Salisbury. Bishop's School represented the Tailors' guild with the Giant and Hob-Nob, but it was the massed numbers of boys and girls (550 by this time) which impressed the town and 'stole the show'. Marching in columns, with the girls wearing white frocks with blue sashes and blue bands on their boaters and the boys in white flannels with school caps and ties, they made an impressive display'.

By the 1920s the pupils were rapidly outgrowing the premises but the girls remained there until 1927 when South Wilts Grammar School for Girls was built on a new site in Stratford Road.

Today, history is repeating itself. Since 1998 joint classes on both sites have been developed at post-16 level with the girls from South Wilts, who are now a welcome and accepted part of the school.

NOTE William Golding, author of the novels *Lord of the Flies* and *The Spire,* winner of the Nobel Prize in Literature, was a schoolmaster here, teaching

The Close, Salisbury

No 11, The Close, Bishop Wordsworth's School, about 1905 (© The Salisbury Museum)

English from 1945 to 1962. *Lord of the Flies*, written in 1954, was Golding's first book, and it is widely believed that many of the characters were loosely based on the boys at the school.

Happold, F C, 1950, (compiled and edited), *Bishop Wordsworth's School 1890-1950,* privately printed for BWS

Davies, R, 1993, *The foundation and early years of Bishop Wordsworth's School,* privately printed for BWS

Robertson, Dora, 1947 (edited from the researches of C R Everett), 'A History of No 11 The Close, Salisbury', *Wiltshire Archaeological Magazine,* vol 5, p307–17

Durman, Richard, 2004, 'The Great Deception: Mathematical Tiles in Salisbury', *Sarum Chronicle 4*

Geraldine Symons (1909–1996)
26 The Close

Geraldine Symons lived in or near the Close almost all her life, and left an evocative picture of her childhood in *Children in the Close* published in 1959 and illustrated by her sister Helen.

Number 26, 'just too tall to be square', drawing Helen Skyrme. See also 54

'Just too tall to be square', No 26 is on the corner of the North Walk and Rosemary Lane. It was built about 1770 as a private house, and this is largely what is seen today, plus some later 19th century extension to the rear. At the time of the book it was covered in Virginia creeper, a subject of fascination for the children. The nursery floor at the top was six flights of stairs from the kitchen in the basement. Coal, water and food had to be carried up and down several times a day.

Outside the house the roads were dusty (laid by a water cart pulled by a horse in a straw hat), the paths were of gravel, and in the days before motor mowers, cutting the grass was 'a gargantuan task literally never finished'.

> *The Daisy Woman, her task as endless as the mower's, spent all her working hours on her knees. Crouched like a nibbling rabbit, she dug up daisy roots with a fork all day long. Small and hump-backed, she wore on her head an old straw hat like a bee hive, darkened by age and exposure to brown. Sometimes when we wandered past her, we stopped to say 'Good morning', then she would rear up a little and say it too, but she was never one for conversation.*

Geraldine Symons grew up here, her grandmother's house, in a very female household. 'Grandmother' was widowed Mrs Bennett (whose father-in-law had owned the *Salisbury Journal*, and whose mother-in-law had continued to run the business after the death of her husband). Then there were two of her daughters, Aunt Baba and Geraldine's mother; Geraldine and her three sisters, Eugenie, Sylvia and Helen, plus Nanny and other domestic staff. The girls' father was in the Army Medical Service, and he with other male relatives visited from time to time, but were never central to the picture.

Geraldine Symons is considered a mistakenly neglected author. Her *Miss Rivers and Miss Bridges* (1971) is a rare piece of children's fiction with a suffrage theme.

Symons, G, 1959, *Children in the Close,* Batsford (second edition 1988 Summers)
Salisbury Journal 13 June 1996 obituary

Edith Olivier (1872-1948)
20 The Close

E dith Olivier was the daughter of Canon Dacres Olivier, rector of Wilton. When he became too infirm for parish duties they moved into the Close in 1912. He was given 'the house earmarked for the senior prebendary' (he held the Prebend of Preston 1874-1919) at No 20 on North Walk.

Amongst the houses of the Close a number were allocated to people holding particular offices in the Cathedral or Diocese. Canons received an income from their prebendal estate, and were expected to maintain periods of residence in the Close, in a household appropriate for offering hospitality to others. No 20 has an elegant symmetrical facade of about 1720, and many original features remain. Parts of an earlier structure were incorporated for the kitchen and offices. Just over a century later a new range was built into the north-west angle of the house. Apart from a new porch of c 1869 little has altered since.

Edith was not keen on the move, but used her powers of observation and skill with words to comment on her neighbours, and their houses, to the benefit of later readers.

> The Close houses seem to have a remarkable effect on their owners. A community mainly consisting of clergymen and old ladies does not sound a promising forcing ground for unusual personalities, yet Salisbury Close has always abounded in these.
> The city outside the Close walls seemed very far away; and when we sat in the garden on summer nights, my father often remarked that it was almost incredible that twenty thousand people could be living a few hundred yards away.

During the First World War one day

> the Close was unexpectedly invaded by swarms of dusty exhausted soldiers. ... Who could they be? Rumours fluttered out from every door. And with them there fluttered out too the Canons' wives and the old ladies, all followed by neat maidservants carrying trays of tea to the tired soldiers. Thus the Close reacted to the trumpets of war. With cups of tea.

After the death of their father in 1919, Edith and her sister Mildred moved first to Fitz House in Teffont, and then, in 1922, to the Daye House in Wilton Park where she lived for the rest of her life.

Edith took on a number of public responsibilities, as organiser of the Women's Land Army in Wiltshire during the First World War, in local parliamentary politics for the Conservative Party, and with the Women's Institute. Although she had been an active campaigner *against* women's suffrage, in 1934 she became the first

Edith Olivier about 1912, from *Without knowing Mr Walkley*, 1938, Edith Olivier

Edith on a day bed at the Daye House, 1942, Rex Whistler (© The Salisbury Museum)

women councillor on Wilton Borough Council and was mayor from 1938 to 1941. Her many additional duties in World War Two included being president of the local St John's Ambulance.

In addition to her public roles, she was an author with over half-a-dozen published books, and was close friend and hostess to members of the artistic circle of a younger generation – Rex Whistler, Cecil Beaton, Siegfried Sassoon, Stephen Tennant, and William Walton - who found peace and sympathetic society at the Daye House. She became particularly close to Rex Whistler who rented the Walton Canonry from 1938 where Edith would have visited him.

Olivier, E, 1938, *Without Knowing Mr Walkley,* Faber & Faber

Jill Furse (1915–1944) and the Whistlers
The Walton Canonry
69 The Close

The Walton Canonry dates from c 1720 and replaced an older canon's residence of which nothing now remains. From 1698 to 1719 the house had belonged to Canon Isaac Walton son of Izaak Walton, author of *The Compleat Angler*. Canon Francis Eyre rebuilt the dwelling and his arms impaling those of his wife, Anne Hyde, can be seen above the front door. One of the most charming houses in the Close its warm red brick façade with stone dressings is welcoming and makes an attractive contrast to its neighbour, the stately Myles Place.

Rex Whistler (1905–1944) saw the house one bright weekend in May. 'Rex crazy for it', wrote Edith Olivier and he described the Close as 'deep, sleepy, quiet all day long, with yellow leaves drifting down and an occasional bell tolling'. He was an artist of astonishing versatility, and Edith Olivier, who must have visited the Walton Canonry frequently, was his confidante and emotional support, and he 'the whole happiness of my [Edith's] life'. When they met, she was in her early 50s and he not quite 20; what developed was an extraordinarily intense friendship which lasted until his death. She was delighted with his tenancy of the Walton Canonry as it brought him geographically nearer to Wilton where she was mayor.

Rex leased the house in 1938 and was based there for much of the following year. It was to be a studio for himself and a home for his elderly parents. His father was increasingly frail and died in the autumn of 1940; his funeral service was held in the Cathedral.

The Walton Canonry 1938, pencil and watercolour (© the estate of Rex Whistler)

Having seen the house in the Close, Rex had to return to make a drawing to send to his mother – 'early Georgian of soft red brick, with a long garden running down to the Avon and the water meadows beyond; so that it seemed to be in Close and countryside at once, with familiar pictures by Constable on every side.' from *The Laughter and the Urn*, 1985, Laurence Whistler

In September 1939 Rex's younger brother Laurence (1912-2000), glass engraver and poet, married the beautiful West End actress, **Jill Furse**. It was arranged by special licence, 'the quietest of cathedral weddings' in the east end of the Cathedral, with Rex acting as best man. The only guests apart from family were Edith Olivier, Siegfried and Hester Sassoon, and David and Rachel Cecil; the reception was held in the Walton Canonry. 'Nothing went wrong' Rex wrote 'except no ice for the champagne, and I did not lose the ring'. Jill and Laurence returned to the house the following Christmas, amidst the uncertainty of the recent declaration of war, but nothing seemed able to mar their sense of contentment with each other.

Jill Furse was the granddaughter of the poet Sir Henry Newbolt from Netherhampton House near Salisbury and, as a frequent visitor, she had a long-

An informal photograph of Jill and Laurence Whistler in 1939 on honeymoon in North Devon. (courtesy of Robin Ravilious)

lasting affection for her 'favourite' city. Described as having 'beauty, sensitivity and talent', her short marriage to Laurence was an intensely happy one, much of it spent in their cottage in North Devon. As an actress she appeared destined for a brilliant career but she suffered from intermittent ill health which affected her London stage roles. She had two children, Simon (1940-2005), and Caroline (Robin) born in 1944. Jill died in November 1944, at a tragically young age, from a recurring blood disorder, (now thought to have been a form of Lupus), shortly after giving birth to her daughter. 1944 was a terrible year for Laurence, losing not only his adored wife, but also his beloved brother Rex who had joined the Welsh Guards and was killed in action in Normandy in July.

The Walton Canonry itself was requisitioned during the war; part of the house was occupied by a small officers' mess and was then sublet to the Commander in Chief for six months. Rex meanwhile renewed the lease for seven years and the idea was mooted by Edith in 1943 that Jill and Laurence would share the house with Rex at the end of the war, with the dwelling divided into two. Jill liked the notion of returning at weekends to the Close from the theatre in the West End. Rex embroidered the vision of 'Whistler's Academy' for small children, 'under a versatile staff of three . . . the main attraction being "a little crockadile to the

Cathedral on Sundays"'". Sadly, just over a year later, only one of the three was living.

Laurence, in homage to Jill, wrote the moving *Initials in the Heart* which chronicled their idyllic five year marriage. She inspired his poetry which recorded both his grief, and his love. Just as he mourned and celebrated Jill so he also perpetuated his brother's memory within his writing and also in his engraved glass. His stunning, revolving glass prism memorial to Rex is one of the treasures of Salisbury Cathedral.

Thanks to Robin Ravilious (née Whistler) for her help and encouragement

Whistler, Laurence, 1965, *The Initials in the Heart,* Rupert Hart-Davis

Whistler, Laurence, 1985 *The Laughter and the Urn: The Life of Rex Whistler,* Weidenfeld & Nicolson

Cecil, Hugh & Mirabel, 2012 *In Search of Rex Whistler, his life and work*, Francis Lincoln

Cecil, Hugh & Mirabel, 2013, *Rex Whistler's Wessex, Landscapes, Friendships, War,* The Salisbury Museum

Musson, Jenny, October 2011, 'Step into the Light', *Country Life,* 108-111

Dora Robertson (1893-1972)
56 and 57 The Close

On the western side of Choristers' Green two adjoining buildings, Braybrooke House and Wren Hall, 57 and 56 The Close, have been long associated with the Cathedral or Choristers School. From the mid 16th century Braybrooke House became the residence of the headmaster, and Wren Hall, as it is now known, was built in 1714 to provide space for a larger schoolroom and other accommodation.

Rev A G Robertson was appointed the new Headmaster in the summer of 1900. Over the next quarter century Mrs Robertson supervised the establishment with great efficiency, and the education and music at the school developed while it expanded in numbers of boys. Sadly in 1924 May Robertson died following a stroke. Shortly afterwards the school required a new matron, and Miss Dora Butterworth was employed to this role. She was to have a short-lived career as school matron, as three months after her arrival the Headmaster and Miss Butterworth were engaged. After their marriage in October 1925, together they ran the school through times both enjoyable and worrying. Problems were overcome, and when A G Robertson retired in 1929 he left a well-established modern Preparatory School.

After her husband's death in 1936 Dora Robertson began the work for which many know of her today, researching and writing the first history of the school. *Sarum Close: A Picture of Domestic Life in a Cathedral Close for 700 years & the History of the Choristers for 900 years* was first published in 1938 (with a second edition appearing in 1969).

Some early steps towards a history had been taken a few decades previously. Clifford Holgate (1859-1903) was Bishop John Wordsworth's legal secretary. He not only kept detailed notes of the daily life of the choristers but also compiled records of his explorations in the archives. He kept in touch with former choristers and added their memories to his notebooks.

Holgate's collection was one source used by Mrs Robertson. She herself contacted former boys, staff and friends of the school asking for their reminiscences, which she used, it is said, somewhat selectively though the complete versions survive. A major part of her own research was in the rich original documents in the Diocesan archives; for example the Chapter Act books, the minute books of the Dean and Chapter which recorded their often anguished deliberations over the choir through the centuries. Holgate's lists aided her with this, but her main help came from Canon Christopher Wordsworth who, as Dora wrote in the dedication of the book 'for five years put his scholarship and historical knowledge at my disposal; who translated all the documents from the Latin; and whose friendship has been an inspiration throughout'.

Sarum Close traces in meticulous detail the long story of the Salisbury choristers from the very earliest times at Old Sarum into the 20th century. But it also peoples the Close with characters of all descriptions, and a surprisingly large number of them are women. Our introduction has mentioned a few of the more colourful ones who participated in the apparently regular disputes over offices and property. Not all were so bellicose: John Taylor was appointed as the teacher of the choristers in September 1569. Sadly less than two years later he died. In

Dora Robertson   Edith Moberly   Elizabeth Vaux

Helen Kingsbury and Lucy Byrne

what Dora Robertson suggests was a unique episode for that time, his widow Alicia attended a Chapter meeting and discussed 'the feeding of the Choristers'. It was agreed that she should provide them with board and lodging for the next three months, for the sum of £10, until a new master was appointed.

Amy Hele, another headmaster's wife, left some little record in addition to her charming epitaph in the Cathedral. Rev Richard Hele ran the school for fifty years in the first half of the 18th century. When Amy died in 1753 she was described as a 'virtuous and good Woman, Blessed with a clear Head, And an honest Heart'. She had written her will 8 years earlier. Amy left the £300 of East India stock inherited from her sister Joanna Collier to her daughter Jane whom she named as her sole executrix, and all three witnesses to the will were women. Jane, who never married, was 38 years old when she went to London to appear before Rt Hon Sir George Lee at the Prerogative Court of Canterbury to take the oath as her mother's executrix.

Of particular importance to the choristers in the 19th and early 20th centuries were four women who, in turn, took a great interest in their education and welfare with a combination of the roles of surrogate aunt, godmother and Sunday School teacher.

Edith Moberly was the third daughter of Bishop George Moberly, so Annie Moberly's older sister. Within the family she was seen as 'the heroine and centre of the house. She was the lively sister who caused things to happen, and suggested all sorts of comings and goings ... a great favourite with the outside world'. For thirty years until into her old age she was a special friend to the Salisbury choristers. Joining in with family life at the Bishop's Palace was a privilege appreciated by the boys as a contrast to the discipline of school. After the Bishop's death Miss Moberly continued to welcome them into her new home in New Street. She went further than Bible teaching and hospitality; for the school she designed the banner and motto, and she was instrumental in establishing links with former choristers.

Miss Elizabeth Vaux took over this role as 'guardian angel to the boys' in the 1890s. She lived in Rosemary Lane with her sister, and there continued the tradition of providing a Sunday afternoon diversion consisting of religious education, readings from literature and lighter volumes, accompanied by

Wren Hall and Braybroke House, coloured postcard 1902 (all illustrations in the chapter from Cathedral School archives)

refreshments. The Misses Vaux and their brother were also financial benefactors to the school, helping at a particularly difficult time.

Succeeding Elizabeth Vaux 1910 came **Miss Helen Kingsbury** and her friend and nurse **Lucy Brine**. As a girl Miss Kingsbury had been disabled as the result of a carriage accident, but Miss Brine had energy for both. The pattern continued of Sunday invitations to their house at No 16 The Close, and there were special treats at Christmas and Easter, when the choristers had to stay at school for services. In summer Miss Kingsbury rented a cottage in Savernake Forest where the boys went on Wednesdays in a 'charabanc'.

For nearly fifty years these women had a hugely beneficial influence on the life of the boys of the choir.

Without Dora Robertson both the choristers and the people around them in the Close would be much less well known and understood. Her meticulous work studying their history over such a long period set a precedent that has hardly been challenged even in modern times.

Smith, Peter L, 2011, *In the Shadow of Salisbury Spire*, Hobnob Press

The Dean and Girl Choristers

The Very Reverend June Osborne (b 1953)

June Osborne was installed as the 80th Dean of Salisbury Cathedral in May 2004 and as such has been promoted as far as the law currently (July 2014) allows within the Church of England. She was the first female dean at a medieval cathedral, and only the second woman after the Dean of Leicester to be appointed to the job. As one of the most senior woman priests she is always among the candidates cited as the possible first female bishop.

One of the initial women to be ordained to the priesthood in 1994, she moved to Salisbury the following year as Canon Treasurer. As a passionate campaigner for equality June Osborne believes that women have brought profound benefits to the church and are now 'sharing leadership naturally with men'.

Following the historic General Synod vote on 14th July 2014 to allow women

June Osborne (courtesy of Salisbury Cathedral © Ash Mills)

Girls' choir (courtesy of Salisbury Cathedral © Ash Mills)

to be ordained as bishops, the Church of England has ended its male domination. June Osborne called it an 'historic day', and once the legal process is complete, women should enjoy full equality within the church, a position for which she has consistently petitioned.

The girl choristers

While boy choristers have been singing at Old Sarum/Salisbury for over 900 years, in 1991 Salisbury became the first English cathedral to recruit a girls' choir. Aged eight to thirteen the 16 girls have a high reputation and enjoy complete equality with the boys. The weekly services are divided between them; only on special occasions do the choristers sing together. They are educated at Salisbury Cathedral School in the old Bishop's Palace.

The choir is frequently involved in BBC broadcasts. A documentary programme about the choristers was shown on BBC television in 2012 with the title *Angelic Voices*; it included episodes in the day to day life of the musically gifted members of both choirs.

The Walking Madonna

Dame Elisabeth Frink (1930-1993) is one of Britain's leading 20th century sculptors, a genuinely popular figure whose work is much admired. She spent the last years of her life near Blandford Forum in Dorset, not far from Salisbury.

The Walking Madonna (1981) is virtually her only female image. She is better known for her large numbers of male figures and animals, especially horses and

The Walking Madonna

dogs. She cared about human rights, was a member of Amnesty International and although not conventionally 'Christian', the 'Walking Madonna' is in the great tradition of religious sculptures around the world, simple but with great dignity. Contemporaries commented on the facial likeness to Frink herself although this may not have been deliberate.

It is a compelling bronze statue showing the older Mary, not the shy, passive Madonna. She is the grieving mother whose son has died but who has to continue with her own life. As Elspeth Moncrieff has written: 'She strides with singleness of purpose … There is an integrity in her gaze … and iron strength in her gaunt frame. Most importantly, she has turned her back on the sanctuary and security of the Cathedral, choosing instead to stride out towards the town to meet the world full on and grapple with the fundamental condition of mankind'.

Mrs Gladys Rattue, steeplejack 1921 (© The Salisbury Museum)

Conclusion

The Close today remains a world within a world. It is still Bishop Poore's 'garden suburb' and would be immediately recognisable by the first women who lived there in the 16th century, having maintained its original design and largely escaped commercial pressures.

Modern Salisbury and the Cathedral Close are inseparable, but the High Street Gate continues to be closed every night, forming an imposing barrier between the bustling city and the privileged territory inside the medieval walls.

A major change is the growth of tourism particularly since the arrival of the railways. Increased numbers of visitors from around the world form a diverse, if transient, community within the Close. But however many people are strolling or hurrying through, there always remains an air of tranquillity and space.

Historically, of greater significance has been the acceptance of a place for women. This owes much to those cultured independent women of the 18th and 19th centuries who quietly got on with their interesting lives, engaged in good works but generally remained in the shadows of their male neighbours.

At Salisbury Cathedral in 2014 there are female canons, vergers, stonemasons, glaziers and conservators. Today there is no longer a feeling of this being 'a community of men'. Women play an equal role within the church and in a real sense take a full part in the society of the Close.

Salisbury Cathedral Close (courtesy of Salisbury Cathedral, © Ash Mills)

Further reading

The following are references for the Close in general or for the lives of several of the women. Additional specific references consulted for each individual woman are given with their biographies.

Everett, Cyril R, *Notebooks* in Salisbury Cathedral Library

Hall, Peter, 1834, *Picturesque Memorials,* Brodie and Co

Hatcher, Henry, 1843, *Old and New Sarum, or Salisbury,* by Robert Benson and Henry Hatcher: Nichols

Heape, R Grundy, 1934, *Salisbury, some architecture in the city and the Close,* Methuen

Howells, J, 2007, *Independent women in public life in Salisbury in the second half of the nineteenth century,* unpublished PhD thesis, Goldsmiths, University of London

Howells, J, and Newman, R, (eds) 2011, *William Small's Cherished Memories and Associations,* Wiltshire Record Society Vol 64

Newman, R and Howells, J, 2000, *Salisbury Past,* PhillimoreOlivier, E, 1945, *Four Victorian Ladies of Wiltshire,* Faber & Faber

Oxford Dictionary of National Biography online

Robertson, Dora, 1969, *Sarum Close,* Firecrest Publishing (originally published 1938, Jonathan Cape).

Ross, C, 2000, *The Canons of Salisbury,* Dean and Chapter of Salisbury Cathedral

Royal Commission on the Historical Monuments of England, 1993, *Salisbury: the Houses of the Close,* HMSO

Royal Commission on the Historical Monuments of England, 1999, *Sumptuous and Richly Adorn'd,* HMSO

Victoria County History of Wiltshire volumes 3 (1956) and 6 (1962)

Index

Index